AF338146

HOW DOES A STAR DIE?

Astronomy Book for Kids
Children's Astronomy Books

Speedy Publishing LLC

40 E. Main St. #1156

Newark, DE 19711

www.speedypublishing.com

Copyright 2017

In this book, we're going to talk about how a star forms and dies. So, let's get right to it!

Even though stars are not alive like animals are alive, they still go through stages of birth, mid-life, and death just like animals do. The process of this cycle is called stellar evolution. The life cycle of a star depends on its mass. The more massive stars die more quickly than the smaller stars.

HOW DOES A STAR FORM?

Between stars in space there is a lot of gas as well as dust. Astronomers call these low-density particles "interstellar matter." Over time, this matter forms clouds. Sometimes as they gather, the density increases and then gravity causes the interstellar matter to contract, eventually forming a protostar.

While the protostar continues to slowly contract, its internal pressure as well as its temperature rise. The increase in temperature is caused by gravitational energy that is released. A protostar is a hot object.

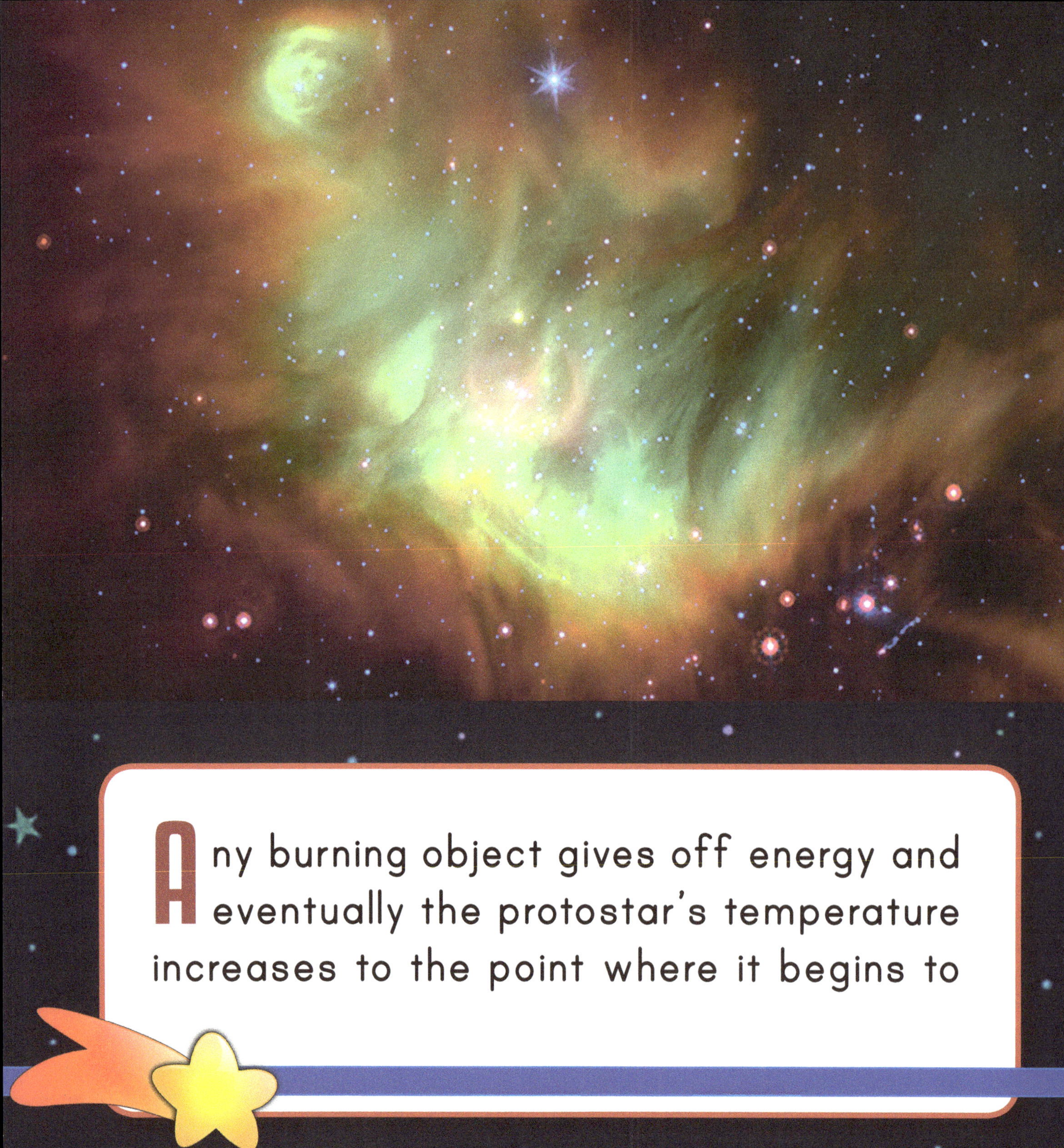

Any burning object gives off energy and eventually the protostar's temperature increases to the point where it begins to

shine. At this point, the temperatures aren't hot enough for nuclear reactions yet.

birth of a star

The pressure continues to build up until it almost equals the force of the gravity. However, as radiation is emitted, it decreases the star's energy. It prevents the interior pressure from completing a balance with gravity. Because of this imbalance, the contraction as well as the heating continue at a slow pace.

The temperature measurement at the protostar's center continues to increase and increase. Finally it reaches a temperature where nuclear reactions begin.

gas and cosmic dust around a young star

That temperature must be 15 million Kelvin in order for the nuclear fusion to start. Once these reactions start, nuclear energy is released. At the beginning, the

star is made up of mostly hydrogen. So, the hydrogen starts to burn and is changed to helium and there are huge energy emissions.

dust disk around a star

When the amount of nuclear energy emitted is in exact balance with the radiation that is lost into the depths of space, the protostar stops contracting. It is in a state of balance and now is a star, making its own energy, heat, and light.

A star that is in a phase of balance with hydrogen reactions taking place within its core has a special name. It's a main sequence star. All stars start their lives in this phase, but not all of them are the same size or brightness level.

hydrogen gas around a star

newborn star

There are three important qualities that are used to categorize what happens to the star next. One is its brightness or luminosity, another is its temperature, and the third is its mass. The sizes of main sequence stars can be plotted on a chart that shows their temperature and brightness. This diagram is called a Hertzsprung-Russell diagram.

If a star in the main-sequence phase has a large mass then it will also be very bright and its surface temperature will be very high.

If a star in the main-sequence phase has a small mass, then it will be very faint and relatively cool compared with much larger stars.

intergalactic star

starburst galaxy

You might think that the biggest stars would stay in the main-sequence phase the longest but the exact opposite is true. The bigger, more luminous stars burn out quicker than the fainter stars.

WHEN IS A STAR NOT MAIN-SEQUENCE ANYMORE

As soon as there's no more hydrogen in the core of the star, it is no longer a main-sequence star. The biggest, most luminous stars are burning their hydrogen reserves faster so they may stop being main-sequence stars in about a million years. For the stars that are not very bright or very big they are burning at a much slower rate and therefore may stay main-sequence stars for trillions of years.

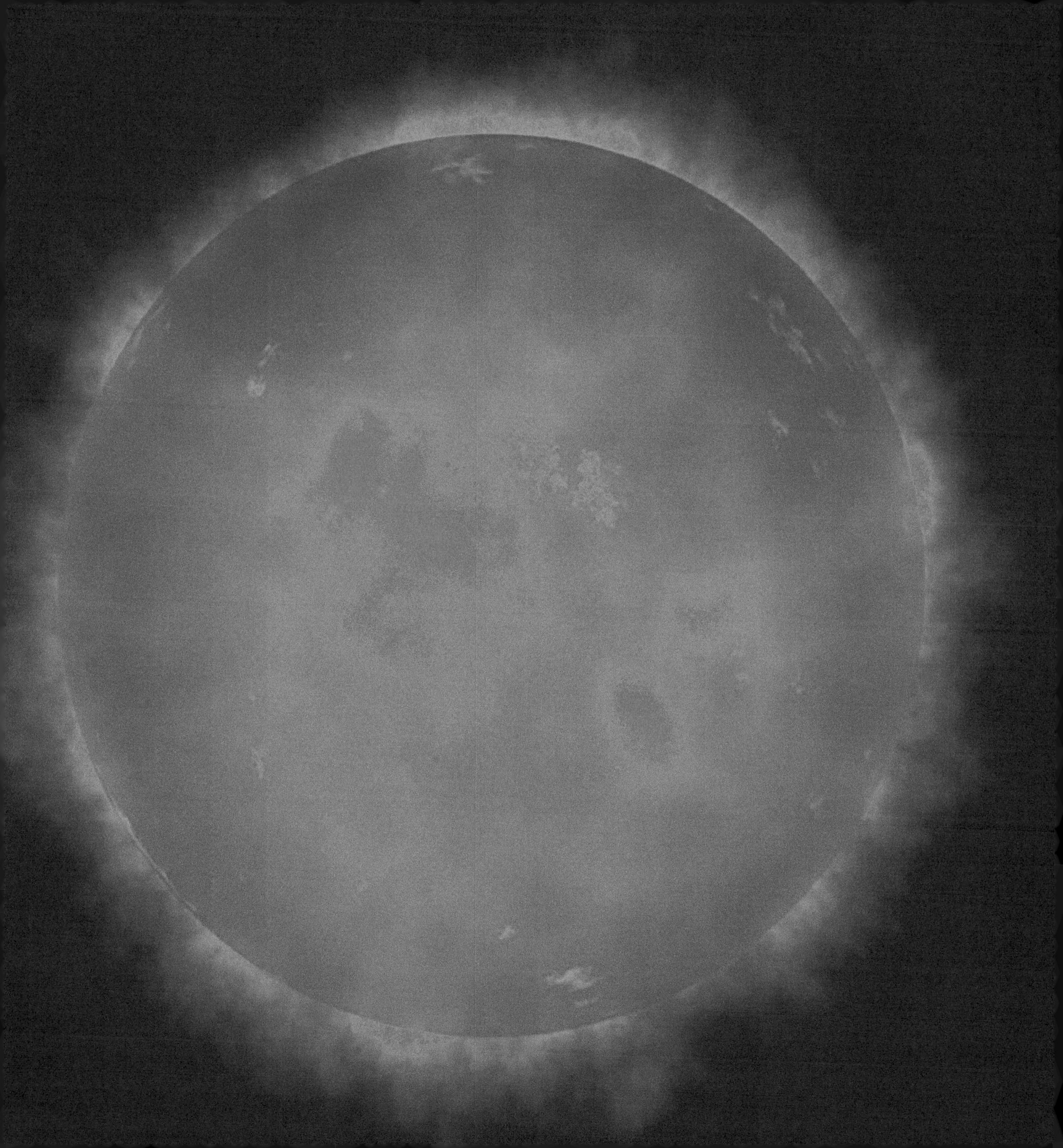

But, in either case, as soon as the hydrogen reserve isn't available, the star isn't a main sequence star anymore. Our star, the Sun, is just about average in size, brightness, and temperature. Astronomers estimate that it will be in the main-sequence phase for about 10 billion (not million) years. It has been around for about 5 billion years, so it has about 5 billion to go.

When all the available hydrogen has gone through nuclear reactions and has changed to helium, nuclear energy is no longer released. The star is no longer in energy balance.

The central core begins to contract down and get even hotter. Even though it doesn't have nuclear reactions anymore, it doesn't mean that the star doesn't shine.

NUCLEAR REACTIONS RESUME

As the core of the star continues to get hotter, the reactions start up again. The core is now helium so the reactions that occur are burning of hydrogen outside the core or burning of helium inside the core. Burning of hydrogen happens at temperatures of around 10 million Kelvin.

However, helium doesn't burn unless the temperature is ten times that amount or 100 million Kelvin. The burning of hydrogen always produces helium, but the burning of helium produces heavier elements such as carbon as well as oxygen. As the elements get heavier and heavier, it requires higher and higher temperatures for nuclear reactions to occur.

eta carinae (massive star)

This second phase of nuclear reactions occur when the star contracts down, the interior heats up, and the hydrogen is now spent. During this time, the outside layers of the star begin to expand.

They cool down compared to the interior and the brightness increases. The star is no longer a main-sequence star, instead it's called a giant or if it's extremely bright, it's called a supergiant.

OLD AGE AND DEATH

As the inner part of the star gets hotter and hotter from the gravitational pull, heavier types of elements will burn. There's a sequence, beginning with helium followed by carbon, then oxygen, then silicon, and so forth. As either the giant star or the supergiant ages, its interior has layers of heavier and heavier elements as it continues to burn. The process doesn't go on forever though.

a Wolf-Rayet star

stellar evolution

In some smaller stars the interior gets so dense that it halts further contractions. This state is called "degeneracy." Eventually, its heat energy dissipates and it turns into a dark, cold body that is called a white dwarf. If it cools to the point where it cannot be seen any longer and fades from view completely, it's called a black dwarf.

White dwarfs have densities that are hard to understand. The density of one cubic centimeter of a white dwarf is measured in tons. A star cannot go into degeneracy or become a white dwarf if it has a mass larger than 1.4 times the Sun's mass. This upper mass for a white dwarf is called the Chandrasekhar limit.

white dwarf

supernova

Stars that have masses larger than this limit, sometimes have powerful explosions that spew out most of the star's material into space with immense force. When a star has this kind of explosion, it's become a supernova.

WHAT HAPPENS DURING A SUPERNOVA?

When a star explodes and becomes a supernova, what's happening is that the core collapses upon itself in a violent spasm. The force breaks off its outer layers and it also breaks down the particles of the core into neutrons.

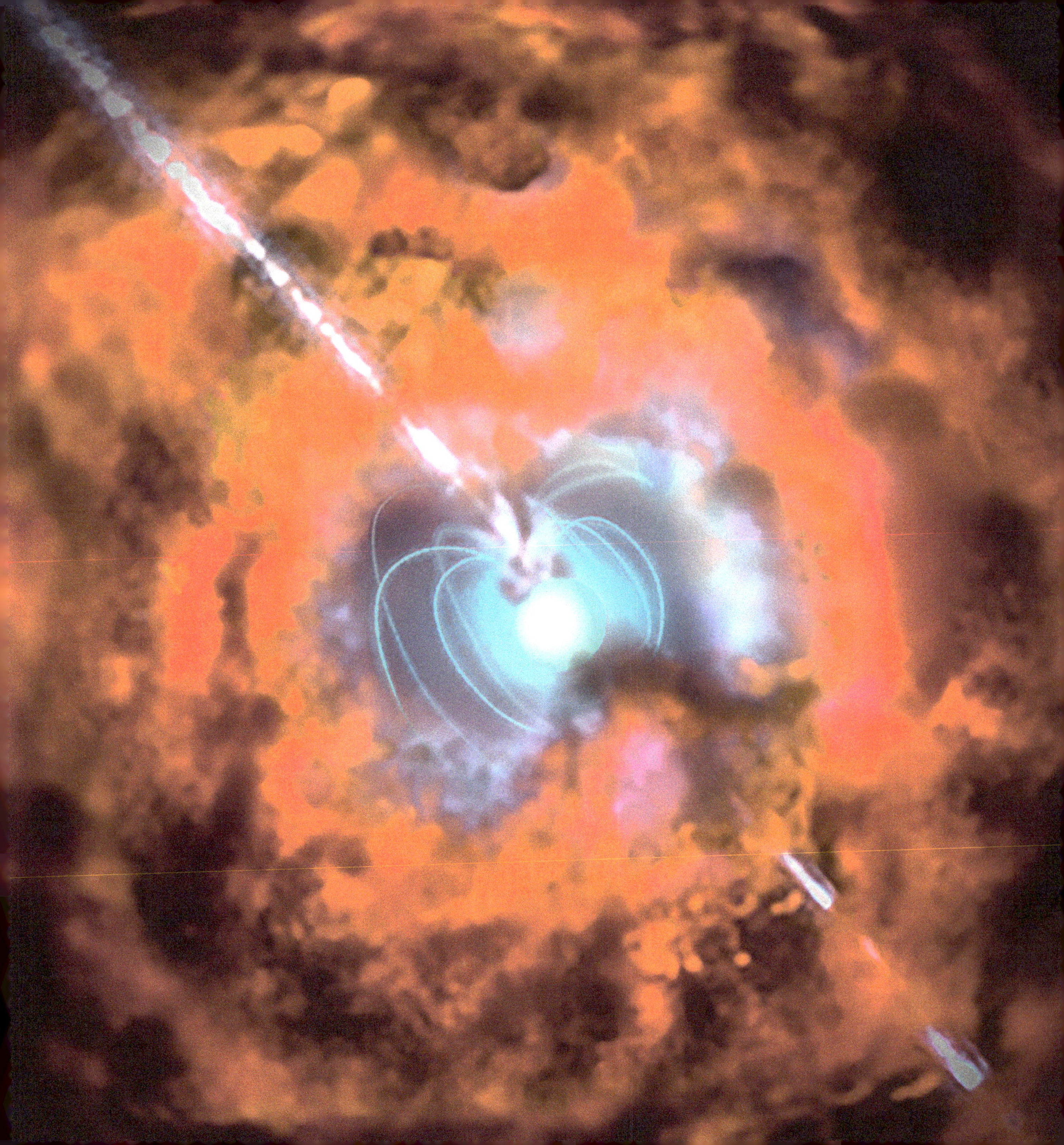

Astronomers have detected some remnants from the explosions of supernovas. They are known as neutron stars. Neutron stars that rotate send out a pulsing signal and that's why they are called pulsars. These stars pulse at about 1,000 times per second. They cannot contract any further, so they end up as dark bodies floating in space.

BLACK HOLE

Sometimes stars don't shed sufficient mass to get to a state of degeneracy. When this occurs, there's nothing to stop the star from contracting and contracting until it gets so dense and small that it becomes a black hole.

black hole Cygnus X-I

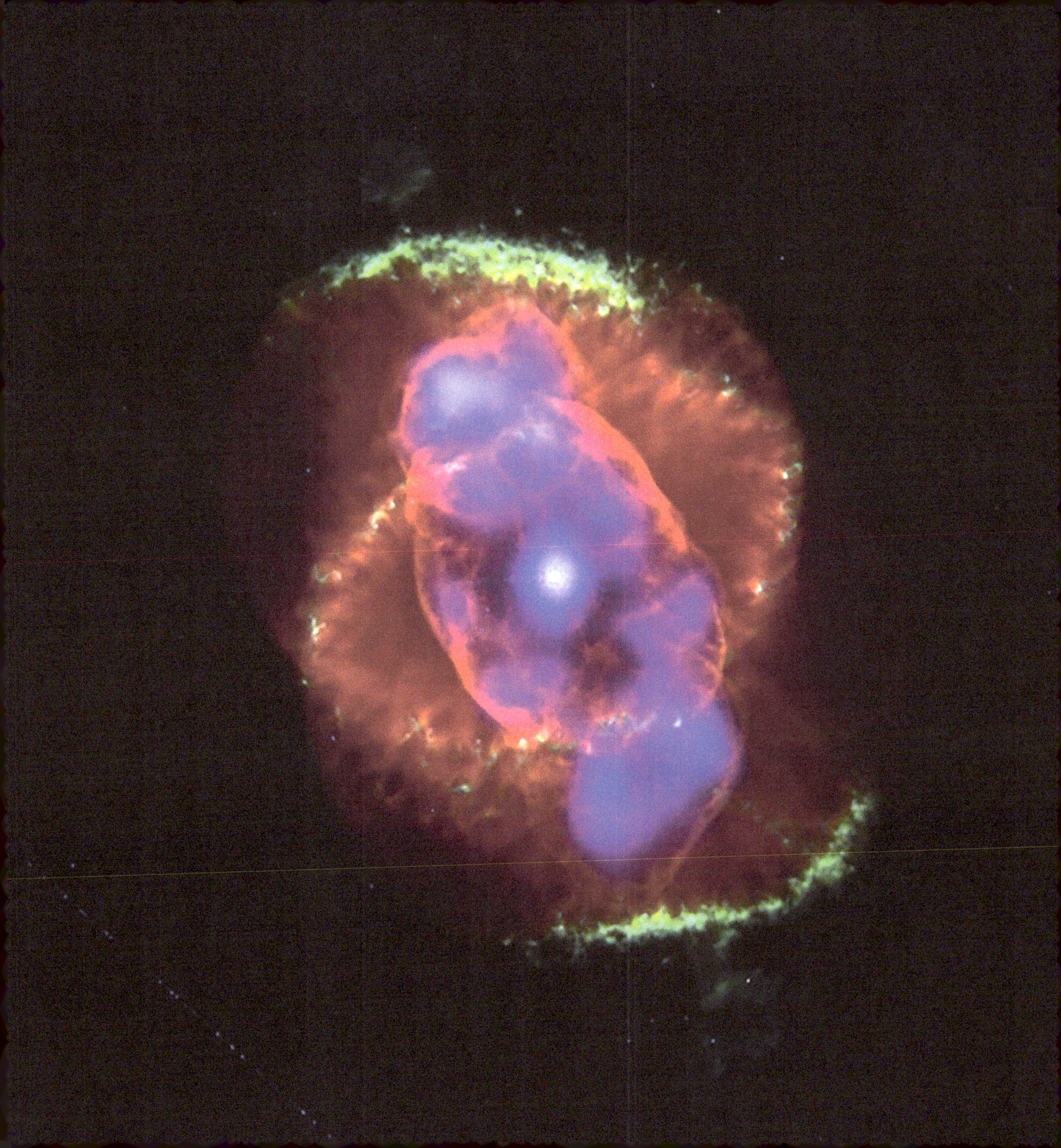

A supernova has so much energy that it can produce very heavy elements like uranium or gold.

Some supernovas have as much luminosity as a whole galaxy, even though it's for a short time.

If the core that remains after a supernova has exploded is more than 5 times the mass of our Sun, then it will collapse to form a black hole.

Because it doesn't create any light, astronomers cannot see black holes. But, they can detect their presence due to the radiation around their edges as well as the immense gravitational pull they have on surrounding objects.

A neutron star contains more mass than our Sun, but its diameter is just a few kilometers wide.

All elements that have atomic numbers larger than the atomic number of lithium have been created by nuclear reactions within stars.

Awesome! Now you know more about the life cycle of a star and how a star dies. You can find more Astronomy books from Baby Professor by searching the website of your favorite book retailer.

9 798869 417060